RISING ABOVE:
PROFILES
IN GREATNESS

TABLE OF CONTENTS

BY LISA BENJAMIN

INTRODUCTION

Public service is employment within a governmental system that aims to benefit the people and their quality of life. That can mean being anything from a forest ranger to a town manager to an environmental coordinator. In many cases, people who have overcome difficult circumstances early in life dedicate their lives to public service. Four such public servants are **Benito Juárez**, **Madeleine Albright**, **Wangari Maathai**, and **Daniel Inouye**. This book is about their contributions.

Benito Juárez *Mexico*
Benito Juárez held many government positions, including president of Mexico. He served five times in that role. As president, he created roads, schools, and reform policies that helped to raise the quality of life in Mexico.

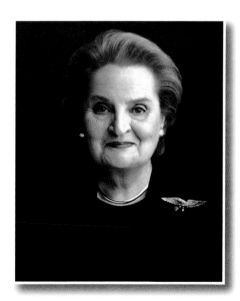

Madeleine Albright *Czech Republic*
As secretary of state, Madeleine Albright strengthened ties between the United States and other countries. She worked for the advancement of human rights and to improve the lives of refugees around the globe.

Wangari Maathai *Kenya*
Wangari Maathai, an environmental activist and women's rights leader, established an organization to provide employment opportunities for women, while making Kenya a greener place.

Daniel Inouye *Hawaii, United States*
Daniel Inouye was a U.S. congressional representative of Hawaii for almost fifty years. His work led to positive change in the lives of many ethnic groups.

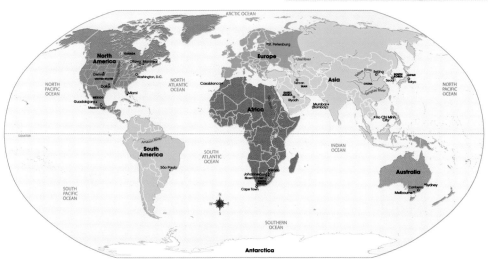

CHAPTER 1:
BENITO JUÁREZ

Benito Juárez (beh-NEE-toh HWAH-res) learned firsthand the difficulties of growing up in poverty. More than 150 years ago, he served five terms as the president of Mexico. Juárez was a Zapotec (zah-puh-TEK) Indian who was born in 1806. His parents, Marcelino Juárez and Brigida Garcia, were peasants. He would later describe them as "*indios de la raza primitiva del pais*," or "Indians of the primitive race of the country."

When Juárez was just three years old, he lost both of his parents due to medical complications from diabetes. After that, he was taken in by his grandparents. After they died, he went to live with an uncle. As a child, Juárez was illiterate. He also could not understand Spanish, the official language of his country. Benito only spoke the language of the Zapotec people.

Benito Juárez grew up in the southern part of Mexico.

At the age of thirteen, Juárez left his community to live with his sister, who worked as a cook. He had to walk forty miles to the city of Oaxaca (wah-HAH-kah), where his sister lived

the city of Oaxaca

and worked as a servant for the Maza family. While living in Oaxaca City, Juárez worked with a bookbinder named Antonio Salnueva (an-TOH-nee-oh sahl-noo-WAY-vuh), who was a friend of the Maza family. Salnueva took Juárez under his wing and became both a mentor and friend to the boy.

Juárez had a strong desire to learn. Salnueva and a local teacher taught him how to speak, read, and write Spanish, as well as how to do arithmetic. The head of the Maza family later sent him to school. Receiving an education was what made it possible for Juárez to change his life, and later the lives of countless others.

He graduated from the Institute of Science and Art in 1843 with a law degree. Even before his graduation, Juárez worked as a city council member in Oaxaca. There he earned a reputation as a strong leader and defender of native rights.

In 1843, Juárez married Margarita Maza. Juárez was thirty-seven and Maza was seventeen.

As a lawyer, Juárez worked to defend and expand the rights of the indigenous peoples of Mexico as well as those who lived in poverty. In fact, he held many political offices, including state legislator and civil judge. Later on in his political career, he became the governor of the state of Oaxaca.

a city center in Oaxaca

As governor of Oaxaca, Juárez was responsible for the construction of new roads and schools. His state government became known for its sense of public spirit and for its honesty. It was this honesty and spirit that would later force Juárez into a brief exile. This was because Juárez voiced his opposition to the corrupt military dictatorship of Antonio Lopez de Santa Anna, who was president of Mexico at the time. During that time, Juárez went to New Orleans, where he worked in a cigar factory. When he returned to Mexico, he served one government, was jailed by another, released and then declared himself president. The United States recognized him as leader. On January 1, 1861, he returned to Mexico City to assume the presidency of a united Mexico.

During the 1850s, two groups fought for control of Mexico's government. Juárez took part in this struggle and helped draft a new **constitution** with a number of **reforms**, or changes. These

ZAPOTEC PEOPLE TODAY

Life has improved for the Zapotec people since the 1800s. They have a rich history and have retained both their language and their culture. Many Zapotec people still live in the state of Oaxaca, working there as farmers, potters, and weavers. Although many make a decent living, others still live in poverty and are among the poorest citizens in all of Mexico. However, thanks to the reforms put in place by President Juárez, Zapotec Indians now have greater opportunities to change their lives than they did long ago.

reforms included the separation of the church from the government. At the time, the Catholic Church had a strong influence over the lives of Mexico's citizens, particularly those living in poverty. The constitution also included a bill of rights and made slavery illegal.

When Juárez became president of Mexico in 1858, the fight over the new constitution grew bigger. This period in Mexico's history, which lasted from 1858 to 1861, is known as the Reform War. When it ended, the reforms Juárez helped draft were put into place and, as a result, conditions improved for many Mexicans. As president, Juárez served a total of five terms. He was the only **indigenous** person ever to achieve this office in Mexico.

Many Zapotec Indians live and work in the state of Oaxaca.

WORDS TO LIVE BY . . .

"The people and the government should respect the rights of all. Among individuals, as among nations, peace is the respect of others' rights."
— Benito Juárez

Benito Juárez was only four feet six inches, one of the shorter presidents in world history. But his height, or lack of it, did not stop him from succeeding. A statue of Juárez stands near a group of highways in Washington, D.C. The statue was a 1969 gift from the Mexican government in exchange for a portrait statue of Abraham Lincoln. Often called the George Washington of Mexico, Juárez is positioned so he is pointing to the bust of Washington

a statue of Benito Juárez in Washington, D.C.

that sits on the campus of nearby George Washington University.

In addition, the United States has statues of Juárez in New York City's Bryant Park, at the Plaza de las Americas on North Michigan Avenue in Chicago, and on Basin Street in New Orleans, where he worked in a cigar factory.

In Mexico, March 21, the birthday of Benito Juárez, is a day that honors his many contributions. There is a city named for him, as well as countless streets, schools, and businesses. Juárez is featured on Mexico's twenty peso bill.

THE LIFE OF BENITO JUÁREZ

1806	1847	1857	1858	1872
Benito Juárez was born on March 21.	He became the governor of Oaxaca.	He helped write a new constitution.	He became the president of Mexico.	Benito Juárez died on July 17.

Today, the people of Mexico celebrate Benito Juárez as a hero, as shown by this sidewalk mural.

CHAPTER 2:
MADELEINE ALBRIGHT

Madeleine Albright achieved great fame and recognition as the first woman to serve as United States secretary of state. When former president Bill Clinton appointed her as secretary of state in 1997, she became the highest-ranking woman in the history of the U.S. government. She said in an interview in 2010, "It took me quite a long time to develop a voice, and now that I have it, I am not going to be silent."

During her time in the position, she worked to strengthen U.S. alliances, advocated for democracy and human rights, and promoted American trade.

But Albright's life did not have a smooth start. She was born in 1937 in the European country of Czechoslovakia, now two countries: the Czech Republic and Slovakia. Like the country of her birth, Albright once had a different name. She was born Marie Jana Korbelova (kor-BEH-loh-vuh). Her grandmother nicknamed her Madeleine when she was a child. She legally changed her first name as an adult. She also married a man named Joseph Albright and took his last name, becoming Madeleine Albright.

Madeleine Albright was born in the city of Prague in the former Czechoslovakia.

Albright was born during a very volatile time in European history. In the 1930s, German **dictator** Adolph Hitler led a political group called the Nazi Party. With the full support of his political party behind him, Hitler declared a state of martial law under the guise of protecting public safety and order. He initiated a countrywide rearmament and set out to form major diplomatic alliances. This seemed to foreshadow future events that would engulf all of Europe in war.

Hitler and the Nazis worked to take over much of the European continent. They occupied many countries including Poland and Czechoslovakia. They also actively **persecuted** the Jewish people. Millions were forced to live and work in inhumane **concentration camps,** or put to death there. Although Albright was raised as a Catholic, she learned later that many of her relatives, including three of her grandparents, were Jewish. They died at the hands of the Nazis. Hitler's genocidal reign of terror set into motion the events that led to World War II.

WORDS TO LIVE BY...

"I was taught to strive not because there were any guarantees of success but because the act of striving is in itself the only way to keep faith with life." —Madeleine Albright

concentration camps places in which people are detained or confined, usually under harsh conditions and without regard to legal norms of arrest and imprisonment

As Hitler rose to power, many Europeans fled their countries. Their goal was to escape the growing influence of Nazi rule. These people became **refugees**, or individuals who were forced to leave their homes due to harsh circumstances. Albright and her family were among the refugees who fled Czechoslovakia, escaping to Great Britain in 1939. This move was difficult for Albright. She suddenly found herself in an unfamiliar place far from home. People spoke a different language and were of an entirely different culture.

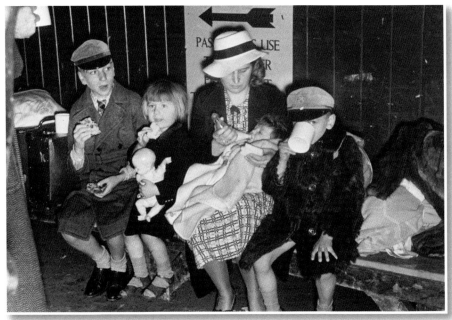

These children were refugees who lived in London during World War II.

Living in a strange place after fleeing home is not easy. It can be particularly difficult for children. It is also very likely that Albright feared for her remaining family back in Czechoslovakia.

Albright's family later returned to Czechoslovakia after World War II ended. Conditions were still far from optimal. Josef Stalin, the **communist** dictator from Russia, had gradually begun to take over the country. Life was very difficult under his harsh rule.

Madeleine Albright was eleven years old when her family was permitted to leave Europe and come to live in the United States. The family settled in Colorado, where her father, Josef Korbel, became the dean of the School of International Relations at the University of Denver. Although she became an American citizen, Albright never forgot the troubles she faced as a child in Europe.

TOUGH TIMES TODAY

Today, about fifteen million people around the world live as refugees. They have left their homes and traveled to the United States or other countries to escape war, terrorism, and persecution. Organizations such as the U.S. Committee for Refugees and Immigrants offer help to make their new lives easier. Organizations provide assistance and opportunities to help refugees find places to live or work, and to help them gain an education.

After graduating from Wellesley College in 1959, she married Joseph Albright. With a master's degree and a Ph.D. in political science from Columbia University in New York City, she headed to Washington, D.C. Madeleine Albright entered politics. She spent many years working for the national government and for the United Nations. In 1996, President Bill Clinton appointed her as U.S. secretary of state. She was the first woman to hold this important office and held the position for four years. As the top American diplomat, her job was to strengthen ties between the United States and other nations. She also worked to help refugees around the globe.

Today, Madeleine Albright is very active. She projects her voice into world affairs and chairs an international consulting firm. She also serves on several boards and is a professor at Georgetown University. She has authored several books.

In an interview about the importance of communicating with people of different perspectives, Albright said, "The thing I learned as a diplomat is that human relations ultimately make a huge difference. No matter what message you are about to deliver somewhere, whether it is holding out a hand of friendship, or making clear that you disapprove of something, the fact is that the person sitting across the table is a human being. The goal is to always establish common ground."

As secretary of state, Albright often met with leaders of other countries such as Benjamin Netanyahu of Israel.

THE LIFE OF MADELEINE ALBRIGHT

1937	1939	1948	1996	2012
Madeleine Albright was born on May 15.	Her family fled Czechoslovakia.	Her family settled in the United States.	She became the first female U.S. secretary of state.	Madeleine Albright released a book called *Prague Winter*.

Of her life, Albright says, "I have had, and continue to have a pretty remarkable life in that I wasn't born in the United States. I came here when I was eleven years old and for me, becoming an American was a major life change. My driving force is that I want to make a difference. I feel that I have been so blessed that it is incumbent upon me to really get in there and make a difference for other people."

Madeleine Albright is grateful for the opportunities that she has had. She has said, "I get up every morning and I go through my list about being grateful for my children and grandchildren, and for the really remarkable life that I have been able to have. I also really do think about the fact that every day counts and I try not to waste it."

CHAPTER 3:
WANGARI MAATHAI

Wangari Maathai was the first African woman to win the Nobel Peace Prize.

Wangari Maathai (wan-GAH-ree mah-TY) is a testament to how **discrimination**—the act of treating people from a certain group unfairly— can be overcome with confidence and determination. Maathai was an environmental activist. She was also a winner of the Nobel Peace Prize. But as a young girl growing up in the African country of Kenya, she often faced discrimination. She was born into a country that regularly put women second to men in terms of power, education, opportunity, and nutrition. In her Nobel Prize acceptance speech in 2004, Wangari remarked that the inspiration for her work came from growing up in rural Kenya.

Maathai was born in 1940, not far from Nairobi (nigh-ROH-bee), the capital of Kenya. Her family members were farmers who taught her to have the deepest respect for nature. As a child, Maathai, like most women and girls in Kenya, faced **gender** discrimination on a consistent basis.

Gender discrimination prevented the women of Kenya from enjoying certain freedoms that many people take for granted. They could only do certain jobs, such as collecting water and gathering firewood, which were seen as jobs that women were supposed to do. Gender discrimination also meant that Kenyan girls were discouraged from attending school.

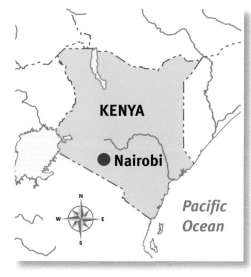

Wangari Maathai grew up not far from Nairobi, the capital city of Kenya.

Despite rampant discrimination, when Maathai was seven years old, she and her brother persuaded their parents to let her go to school. She was a bright girl and a star student, who quickly developed a love for learning. Her teachers encouraged her to pursue further education.

In the 1960s, Maathai left Kenya to attend college and graduate school in the United States. That's where she earned degrees in science. She became the first woman from East and Central Africa to earn a Ph.D., which is one of the highest degrees a student can attain.

Although Wangari Maathai, or Dr. Maathai, as she was addressed by many, enjoyed attending school in the United States, she missed her home and decided to return to Kenya. She wanted to do something to bring about positive changes

One of the schools Maathai attended in the United States was the University of Pittsburgh.

in her country. And, since she was so protective of the environment, she founded the Green Belt Movement. This organization worked with women's groups and planted an estimated forty-five million trees across Kenya.

Maathai created the Green Belt Movement for several reasons. She wanted to do something to help the women of her country and to provide them with new jobs and the kind of opportunities she had been given. The respect for nature that her parents instilled in her also played a part. She wanted to preserve and protect nature because she believed that there is an important link between world peace and the environment.

THE STORY OF THE HUMMINGBIRD

Maathai often retold a fable about a huge fire in the forest. All the animals gathered to watch the flames. But a little hummingbird said, "I'm going to do something about this fire." So he flew to a nearby stream and began to transport water in his beak to the fire. He kept doing this as a crowd of animals just stood and watched. Finally, an elephant said, "You're too little to do much to put the fire out, Hummingbird." But the hummingbird said, "I'm doing the best I can." According to Maathai, that is what we all need to do. "We can't just watch the planet go down the drain," she said.

Her work was controversial. Many men in power saw her as a threat. At times, throughout her life, she had to go underground. In addition to being arrested, she was hit with tear gas, and beaten by the police. Of this, she said in a 2005 interview, "I knew that I was not doing anything wrong. I knew in my mind that I was doing the right thing. I knew that the people who were going against me were not going against me for a good purpose. I knew that they were trying to justify their corruption and misgovernance."

Maathai founded the Green Belt Movement in 1977 to help women and the environment.

At the time the Green Belt Movement was founded, corporations were cutting down trees for manufacturing while people were cutting them down for firewood. This stripped the forests and left them bare. To help repair the environment, the Green Belt Movement planted more trees. The brunt of the work was done by women, which gave them a chance to earn money.

The organization's efforts were not restricted to Kenya, however. The Green Belt Movement soon spread to other parts of Africa. Maathai's efforts made a big difference, and she began to gain honors and recognition. In 2004, she was the first African woman to receive the Nobel Peace Prize.

She was described as a "force of nature," by the executive director of the United Nations program, Achim Steiner. He compared her to Africa's acacia trees, "strong in character and able to survive sometimes the harshest of conditions."

Wangari Maathai became one of the most widely respected women on the continent.

TOUGH TIMES TODAY

Life has improved somewhat in Kenya, but women and girls still face hard times there. They still have limited access to both education and health care. The constitution and laws of Kenya also block women from demanding their rights and bringing about reforms. Although girls and women continue to face discrimination, the Green Belt Movement and other programs have helped improve their lives and will continue to work toward changes in the future.

She played many roles—environmentalist, feminist, politician, college professor, human rights advocate, and head of the Green Belt Movement.

Former Vice President Al Gore said of her, "Wangari overcame incredible obstacles to devote her life to service to her children, to her constituents, to the women, and indeed all the people of Kenya."

THE LIFE OF WANGARI MAATHAI

Wangari Maathai won the Nobel Peace Prize in 2004.

1940	1976	1977	2004	2011
Wangari Maathai was born on April 1.	She joined the National Council of Women of Kenya.	She founded the Green Belt Movement.	She won the Nobel Peace Prize.	Wangari Maathai died on September 25.

WORDS TO LIVE BY. . .

"Every person who has ever achieved anything has been knocked down many times, but all of them picked themselves up and kept going, and that is what I have always tried to do." —Wangari Maathai

CHAPTER 4:
DANIEL INOUYE

Like Madeleine Albright, Daniel Inouye (IH-noh-ay) was greatly affected by World War II. He came of age in a nation that treated him, his family, and his peers with prejudice. His sense of loyalty and duty, however, allowed him to overcome prejudice and led him to a life of public service.

Inouye's lifetime of service included military honors and a long career as a leader in the U.S. Congress. A war hero, Inouye also became the highest-ranking Asian American government official in U.S. history.

Daniel Inouye was born September 7, 1924, in Honolulu, Hawaii. His family had emigrated, or moved, from Japan in search of opportunity. They found work on the islands' sugar plantations. The plantations were owned by whites from the mainland, who had gained political power over native Hawaiians.

Daniel Inouye served in the U.S. Senate for nearly fifty years.

From a young age, Inouye showed an interest in helping people. After surgery for a wrestling injury in middle school, he decided he wanted to become a surgeon. When he enrolled in college, Inouye was a premed student at the University of Hawaii and a Red Cross volunteer.

Many Japanese American families were sent to live in internment camps during World War II.

Inouye was among the first to treat injured soldiers when Japanese fighters bombed the U.S. naval base at Pearl Harbor in 1941. He tried to enlist in the army, but was rejected because the government labeled Americans of Japanese descent as "enemy aliens." The government assumed they would be loyal to Japan instead of the United States. Many Japanese were sent back to Japan, and more than 100,000 people of Japanese ancestry were sent to **internment camps**.

Feeling a sense of duty, Inouye and others petitioned President Franklin D. Roosevelt for the right to enlist. As the need for soldiers grew, the army lifted its ban. Inouye joined the 442nd Infantry Regimental Combat team. It was made up of *nisei*, or Americans of Japanese descent.

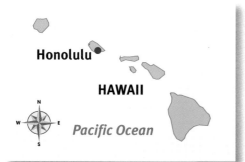

Daniel Inouye was born in the islands of Hawaii.

internment camps places where people are imprisoned or confined for preventive or political reasons, often within their own country

Daniel Inouye entered the U.S. Army in 1943.

At the age of 20, Inouye was promoted to lieutenant and was awarded the Bronze Star. He almost died fighting in France when a bullet struck his chest. His life was saved by two silver dollars he carried in his shirt pocket.

On April 21, 1945, near the war's end, Inouye faced his biggest challenge yet. He led a platoon in attacking the Germans at a ridge named Colle Musatello near San Terenzo, Italy. Germans in machine-gunner nests shot at Inouye and his men. He hurled two grenades to destroy one nest. He used a machine gun to knock out a second, only to be hit by a sniper. Yet, he kept up the attack. An enemy grenade shattered his right arm. Despite intense pain, he kept leading his men in the fight. They neutralized their German targets.

The military doctor didn't think he would survive, but Inouye insisted on treatment. His right arm was amputated. Even with this disability, he stayed in military service until 1947. He was awarded the Distinguished Service Cross, a less prestigious commendation than the Medal of Honor. (Members of Inouye's regiment were denied the higher honor due to their race. President Bill Clinton presented the Medal of Honor to Inouye and twenty-one other Asian American soldiers in 2000.)

Despite coming home a war hero, Inouye still faced prejudice. Even while wearing his uniform, he was refused service by a barber who used a derogatory term for the Japanese.

Inouye couldn't become a surgeon, so he committed to public service and the cause of equal rights. He took part in grass-roots protests designed to shift power away from Hawaii's sugar plantation owners and back to the native peoples. He graduated from the University of Hawaii in 1950 and George Washington University Law School in 1953.

After law school, Inouye became an assistant public prosecutor in Honolulu. He served as majority leader of the territorial Hawaii House of Representatives (1954–1958) before joining its Senate in 1959. That year, when Hawaii became a state, Inouye became its first congressional representative. He was elected senator in 1962, a position he held until his death in 2012.

WORDS TO LIVE BY. . .

"This is my country. Many of us have fought hard for the right to say that. Many are now struggling today from Harlem to Da Nang that they may say this with conviction. This is our country."
— Daniel Inouye

There were two major areas Inouye focused on in his lengthy career in Congress. One was oversight—making sure that government resources are used properly and laws are followed. This included high-profile roles examining the Watergate scandal and the Iran-Contra affair.

Inouye's other focus was fighting for the equal rights of different ethnic groups. He built on his wartime experience trying to make sure Japanese Americans received fair treatment and had equal opportunities to serve. Inouye fought for the rights of Japanese Americans who had been interned during the war, and for Filipino and Filipino American veterans. He also fought for Native Americans while serving on the Committee on Indian Affairs. In that role he helped establish the Smithsonian's National Museum of the American Indian in Washington, DC.

Inouye worked to pass the Civil Liberties Act of 1988, which gave reparations of $20,000 each to those interned during World War II who were still alive. The Act acknowledged that internment was the result of "race prejudice, war hysteria, and a failure of political leadership."

In addition to civil rights, other causes Inouye supported included organized labor, consumer rights, and environmental protection. He owed his long tenure in Congress—he was reelected eight times—to his ability to speak eloquently and persuasively. He worked to get laws passed that brought funding for projects to help Hawaii's economy.

In 2010, Inouye became the Senate's longest-serving member. As was customary, he was named president pro tempore, placing him third in line of succession to the presidency. At the time, that made him the highest-ranking Asian American in U.S. history.

Daniel Inouye was still serving the public at the time of his death (December 17, 2012). Shortly thereafter, on November 21, 2013, he was awarded the Presidential Medal of Freedom, the nation's highest civilian honor. Together with his Medal of Honor, it stood as a testament to Inouye's lifetime of public service and his ability to overcome difficulties.

In 2000, Inouye received the Medal of Honor from President Bill Clinton.

THE LIFE OF DANIEL INOUYE

"Americanism is not and has never been a matter of race or color. Americanism is a matter of mind and heart."

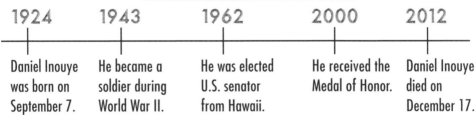

1924	1943	1962	2000	2012
Daniel Inouye was born on September 7.	He became a soldier during World War II.	He was elected U.S. senator from Hawaii.	He received the Medal of Honor.	Daniel Inouye died on December 17.

Upon Inouye's death, President Obama said of him, "He worked to hold those of us in government accountable to the people we were elected to serve, but it was his incredible bravery during World War II, including one heroic effort that cost him an arm, but earned him the Medal of Honor, that made Danny not just a colleague and a mentor, but someone revered by all of us lucky enough to know him."

CONCLUSION

A public servant may focus on a variety of issues that affect society, such as natural resources, education, welfare, or the environment. The issues are all very different, but the public servant remains committed to the cause.

The contributions of Benito Juárez, Madeleine Albright, Wangari Maathai, and Daniel Inouye have helped to improve the lives of many people. Their work has paved the way for other public servants to continue striving for better laws, policies, and overall conditions.

This statue of Benito Juárez stands in Chicago and serves as an inspiration for the people of the city.

Wangari Maathai met with then-senator Barack Obama in 2006.

American politician Margaret Chase Smith said, "public service must be more than doing a job efficiently and honestly. It must be a complete dedication to the people and to the nation."

GLOSSARY

communist (KAHM-yuh-nist) *adjective* following the ideals of communism, a system of government run by a small authoritarian group (page 13)

constitution (kahn-stih-TOO-shun) *noun* a plan for a government (page 7)

dictator (DIK-tay-ter) *noun* a leader who holds complete control over a government or group (page 11)

discrimination (dis-krih-mih-NAY-shun) *noun* the act or practice of treating people from a certain group harshly or unfairly (page 16)

gender (JEN-der) *adjective* related to being female or male (page 17)

indigenous (IN-DIH-jeh-nes) *adjective* native; of a particular region (page 7)

persecuted (PER-sih-kyoo-ted) *adjective* caused a person or a group of people to suffer (page 11)

reforms (rih-FORMZ) *noun* changes designed to right wrongs in society (page 7)

refugees (REH-fyoo-jeez) *noun* people who leave their country or community to escape war, danger, or other problems (page 12)

INDEX

ANALYZE THE TEXT

QUESTIONS FOR CLOSE READING

Use facts and details from the text to support your answers to the following questions.

On page 8, the author describes Benito Juárez's life in politics. Which achievements does the author include?

On page 12, the author explains that it can be difficult for a young refugee to live in a new place. What details support this idea?

On page 22, the author compares Daniel Inouye to Madeleine Albright. What comparison does the author make?

On page 18, the author explains that Wangari Maathai founded the Green Belt Movement for several reasons. What details does the author provide to support this idea?

COMPREHENSION USING TEXT OR GRAPHIC FEATURES

An author can include text and graphic features to provide additional information about a topic. Identify one example of each type of feature in this book and describe the information it provides. Use a three-column chart to help organize your ideas.

Page Number	Feature Type	Information